# LOOK AND SEE 1

## ACTIVITY BOOK

**NATIONAL GEOGRAPHIC**
LEARNING

Australia • Brazil • Mexico • Singapore • United Kingdom • United States

# LOOK AND SEE 1

## ACTIVITY BOOK

**1** TR: **0.1**  Listen and point.

**2** TR: **0.2**  Sing and do.

**STRUCTURE:** *What's your name? My name's Jian.*

**3** Draw and say.

# 1 HELLO!

**1** TR: 1.1 Listen. Circle ✔ or ✘.

**1**  (✔) ✘

**2** ✔ ✘

**3** ✔ ✘

**4** ✔ ✘

**5** ✔ ✘

**6** ✔ ✘

**2** Point and say.

**1**

**2**

**3**

**NEW WORDS:** *Hello! Goodbye. Say hello. Wave goodbye. Stand up. Sit down. Open your book. Close your book.*

# **1** TR: 1.2 Listen and circle.

**1**

**2**

**3**

**STRUCTURE:** *How are you? I'm fine, thank you.*

**1** TR: 1.3 Sing and point.

**2** Look and circle.

 **VALUE** MAKE FRIENDS.

**1**

**2**

**SONG AND VALUE:** *Make friends.*

**1** Trace.

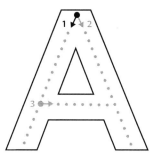

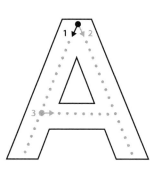

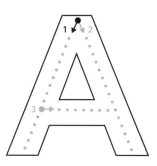

**2** Draw yourself.

**1** TR: 2.1  Listen and circle.

**1**

**2**

**3**

**4**

**5**

**6**

**1** TR: 2.2 Listen. Circle ✔ or ✘.

**1** ✔ ✘  **2** ✔ ✘  **3** ✔ ✘  **4** ✔ ✘  **5** ✔ ✘

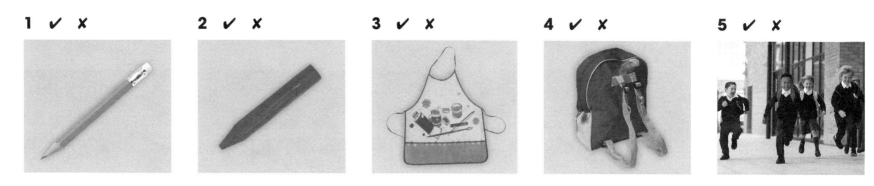

**2** Color. Ask and answer.

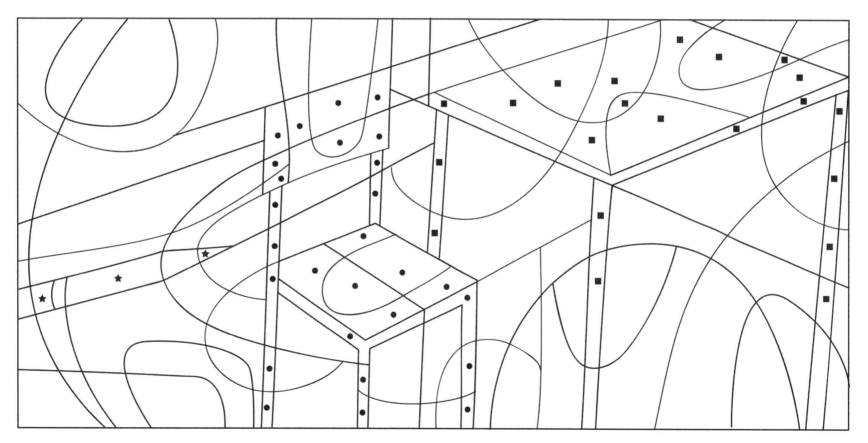

**STRUCTURE:** *What's this? It's a pencil.*

**11**

**1** TR: 2.3 Color. Sing and point.

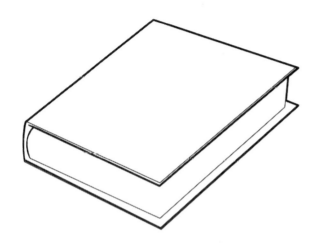

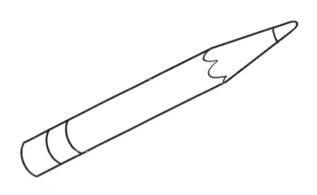

**2** Look and circle.

VALUE  TAKE CARE OF YOUR THINGS.

**1**

**2**

**1** Trace.

**2** Draw your school.

# UNIT 3 COLORS

**1** TR: 3.1 Listen and color.

**NEW WORDS:** *blue, green, orange, paint, purple, red, yellow*

**1** TR: 3.2 Listen and color. Then ask and answer.

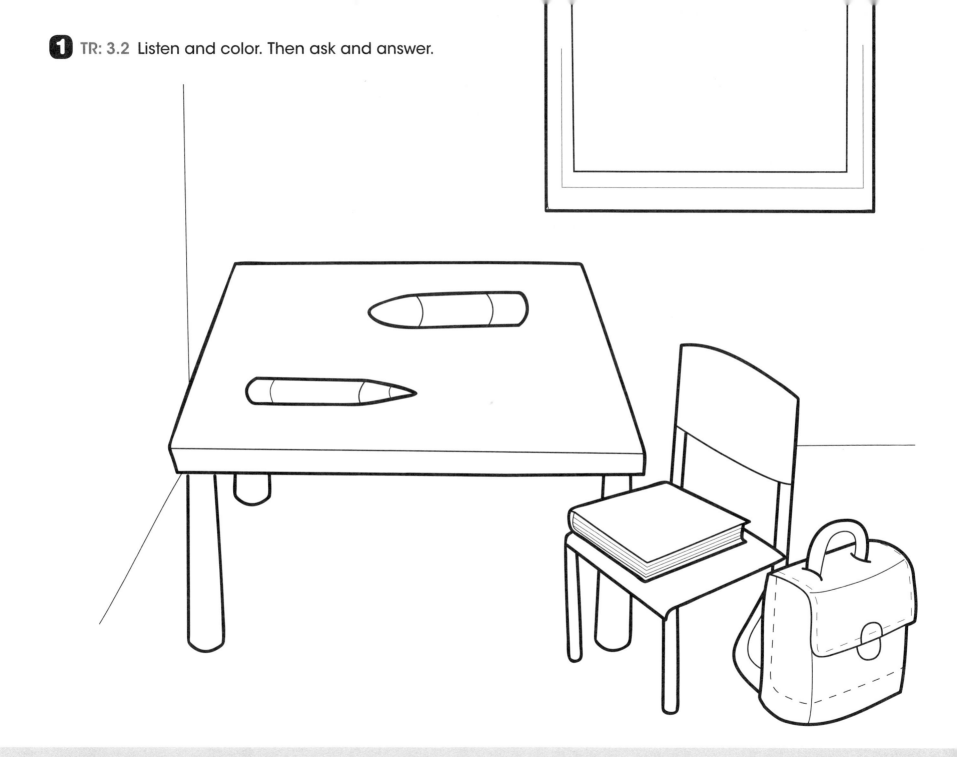

**1** TR: 3.3 Color. Sing and point.

**2** Look and circle.

**VALUE** BE CREATIVE.

**1**

**2**

**1** Trace.

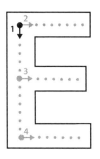

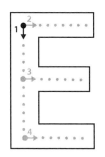

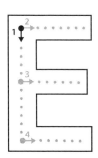

**2** TR: 3.4 Listen and color.

**1**

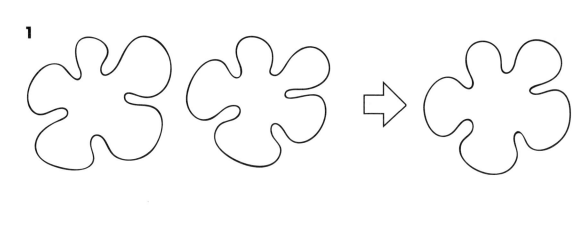

**2**

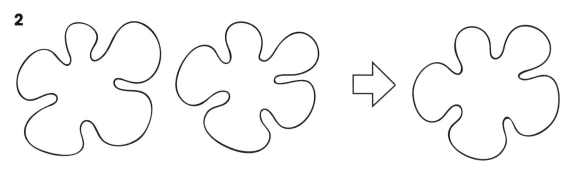

**3**

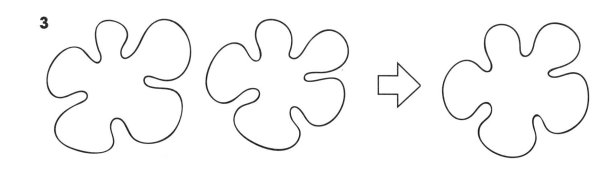

**1** TR: 4.1 Listen. Circle ✔ or ✘.

1 (✔) ✘     2 ✔ ✘     3 ✔ ✘

4 ✔ ✘     5 ✔ ✘     6 ✔ ✘

**2** Color. Then point and say.

1

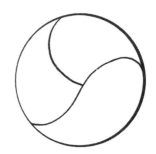

2

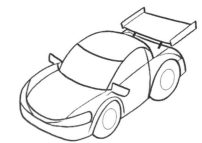

3

**NEW WORDS:** *ball, bus, car, doll, puppet, teddy bear, train*

**1** TR: 4.2 Listen and circle.

**1**

 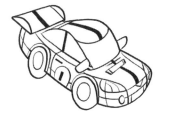 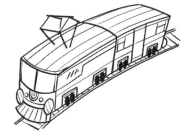

**2**

**1** TR: 4.3 Listen, point, and count. Then color.

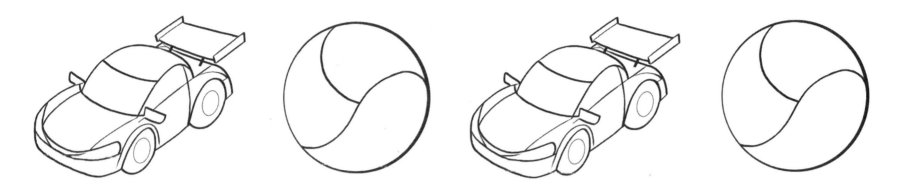

**2** Look and circle.

**VALUE** SHARE YOUR TOYS.

**1**

**2**

**1** Trace.

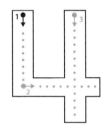

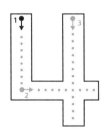

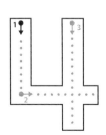

**2** Draw your favorite toy.

# UNIT 5 LET'S MOVE!

**1** TR: 5.1 Listen and point.

**2** Trace and say. Then color.

**NEW WORDS:** *arms, body, feet, hands, head, legs, tummy*

**1** Play and say. Then do.

 HEADS: MOVE 1

 TAILS: MOVE 2

**START** →

 MOVE BACK

 ← 1  **FINISH** ★

STRUCTURE: *Touch your head. Move your hands.*

**1** TR: 5.2 Listen and color. Then sing.

**2** Look and circle.

VALUE    BE ACTIVE.

1

2

**1** Trace.

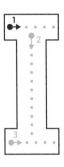

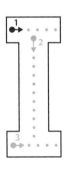

**2** TR: 5.3 Listen and point.

**1**

**2**

**3**

**1** TR: 6.1 Listen and circle.

**1**
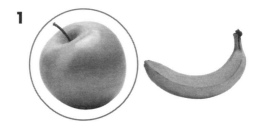

**2**

**3**

**4**

**5**

**6**

**2** Color. Then point and say.

**NEW WORDS:** *apple, banana, carrot, cracker, milk, orange, water*

**1** TR: 6.2 Listen and circle.

**1**

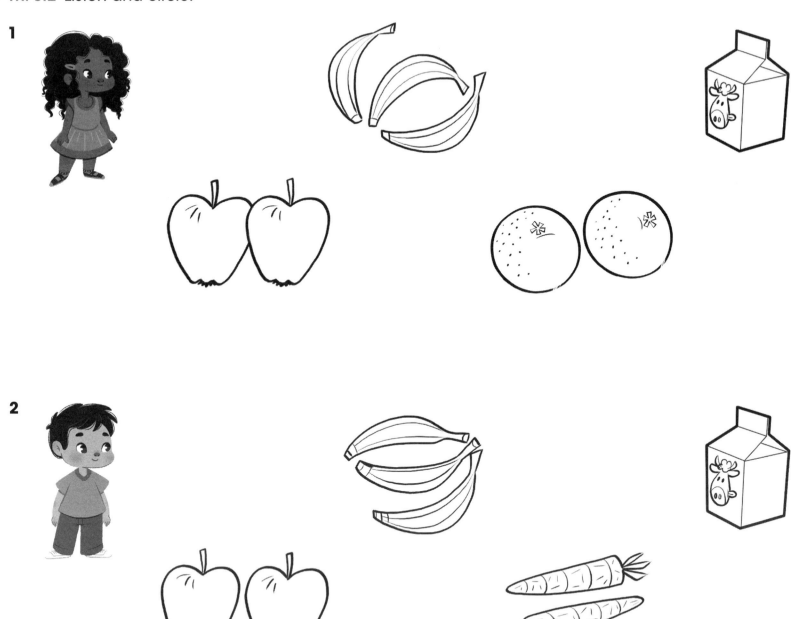

**2**

**1** TR: 6.3 Listen and color. Then sing and point.

**2** Look and circle.

**VALUE** CHOOSE HEALTHY FOOD.

**1**

**2**

**1** Trace.

**2** Draw your favorite tree.

# MY FAMILY

**1** TR: 7.1 Listen and match.

**1**

**A**

**2**

**B**

**3**

**C**

**2** Point and say.

**NEW WORDS:** *brother, dad, grandma, grandpa, mom, photo, sister*

**1** Draw your family and say. Then color.

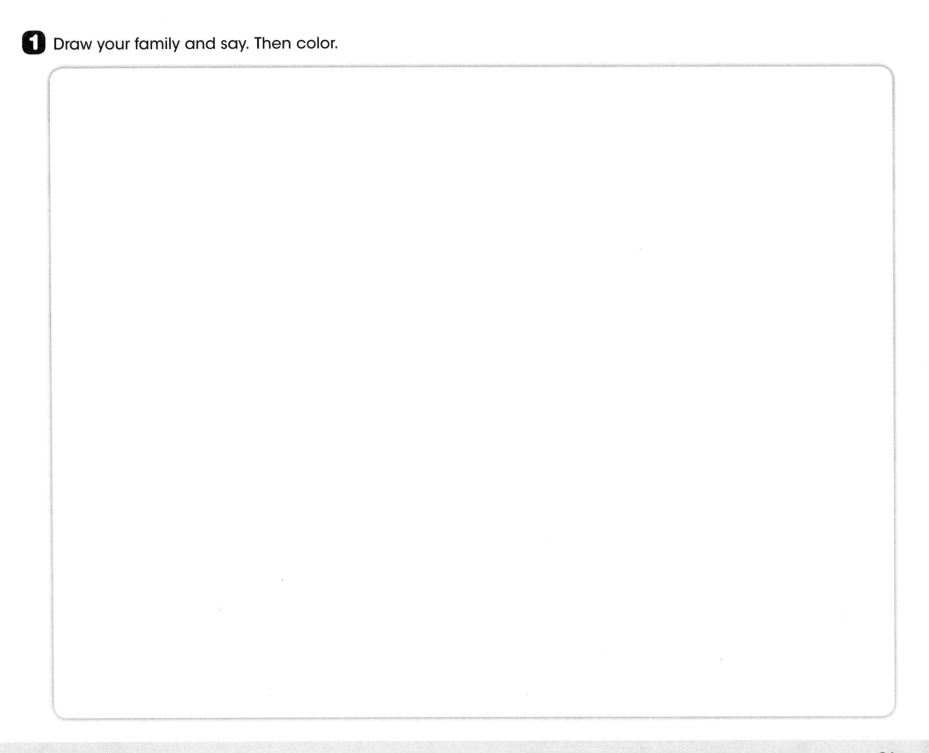

**1** TR: 7.2  Listen and match. Then sing.

**2** Look and circle.

 **VALUE** **BE GOOD TO YOUR FAMILY.**

**1**

**2**

**3**

**1** Trace.

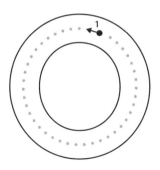

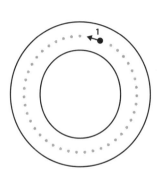

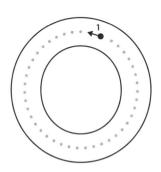

**2** TR: 7.3 Listen and match.

# 1  2

# ON THE FARM

**1** TR: 8.1 Listen. Circle ✔ or ✘.

**1** ✔ ✘    **2** ✔ ✘    **3** ✔ ✘    **4** ✔ ✘    **5** ✔ ✘    **6** ✔ ✘    **7** ✔ ✘

**2** Match and say.

**1**   **2**   **3**   **4**

**A**   **B**   **C**   **D**

**34**    **NEW WORDS:** *cat, chicken, cow, dog, goat, horse, sheep*

**1** TR: 8.2 Listen. Circle ✔ or ✗.

1 ✔ ✗

2 ✔ ✗

3 ✔ ✗

4 ✔ ✗

5 ✔ ✗

**2** Ask and answer.

1

2

3

4

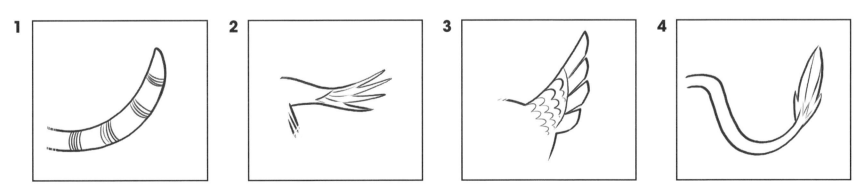

**1** TR: 8.3 Sing and point.

**2** Look and circle.

TAKE CARE OF ANIMALS.

**1**

**2**

**3**

**1** Trace.

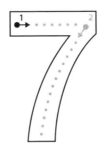 

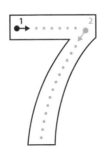 

**2** Match and say.

**1**

**A**

**2**

**B**

**3**

**C**

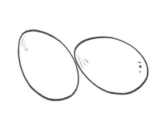

**1** TR: **9.1** Listen and match.

# 1 2 3 4 5 6

**2** TR: **9.2** Listen and color.

1  2  3  4  5  6

**NEW WORDS:** *hat, jacket, shoes, shorts, socks, T-shirt; black, brown, white*

**1** TR: **9.3** Listen and color. Then match and say.

**1** TR: 9.4 Listen and color. Then sing.

**2** Look and circle.

**DRESS YOURSELF.**

**1**

**2**

**3**

**1** Trace.

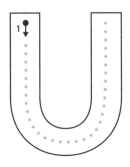

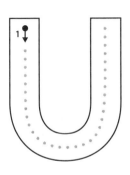

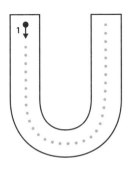

**2** Trace, match, and say.

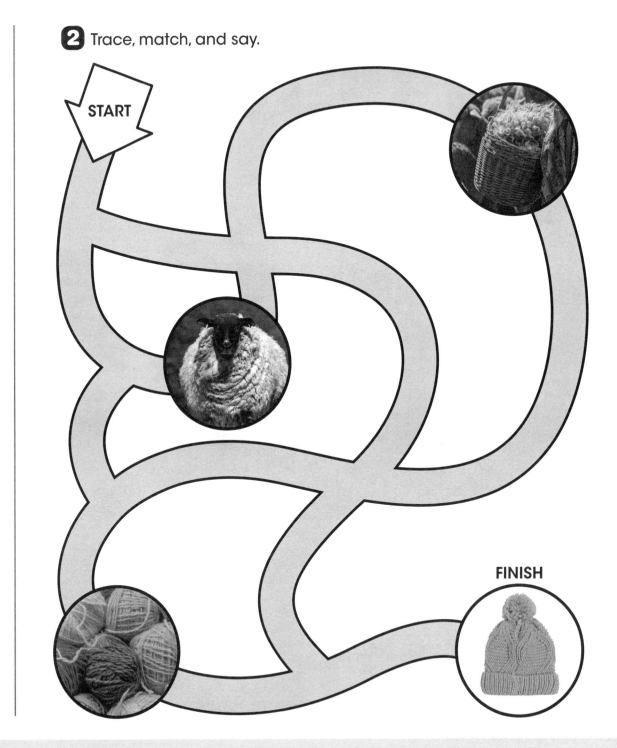

START

FINISH

**1** TR: 10.1 Listen and circle.

**1**

**2**

**3**

**4**

**5**

**6**

**2** Point and say.

**1** TR: 10.2 Listen and circle. Then find.

1 2 3

1 2 3

1 2 3

4 5 6

4 5 6

6 7 8

6 7 8

**STRUCTURE:** *How many birds? Four birds.*

**1** TR: 10.3 Listen and circle. Then sing.

# 1 2 3

# 3 4 5

**2** Look and circle.

VALUE    EXPLORE OUTSIDE.

**1**

**2**

**3**

**1** Trace.

**1**

**2**

**3**

# CREDITS